ME TOO!
B O O K S

"Now I See"

THE STORY OF THE MAN BORN BLIND

By Marilyn Lashbrook

Illustrated by Stephanie McFetridge Britt

RAINBOW
STUDIES
INTERNATIONAL

El Reno, Oklahoma

The book "NOW I SEE" tells the
story of a blind man who receives
his sight and much more. Young
children often respond to handicaps
with curiosity and compassion. To
help your little one understand
blindness, turn off the lights at
night for a minute as you talk about
the man who never saw anything
but darkness. As you read the story,
pause at the designated words and
allow your child to say the word
and/or point to the picture. (As
your child grows, let your child read
more and more of the story to you.)
This story will help your child learn
about God's love and His desire to
heal our hurts. Your little one will
also learn that it is not enough just
to know about Jesus. We must
respond to Him with faith
and obedience.

ISBN 0-933657-62-5

Art direction and design by
   Chris Schechner Graphic Design

ME TOO!
B O O K S

"NOW I SEE"

THE STORY OF THE MAN BORN BLIND

By Marilyn Lashbrook

Illustrated by Stephanie McFetridge Britt

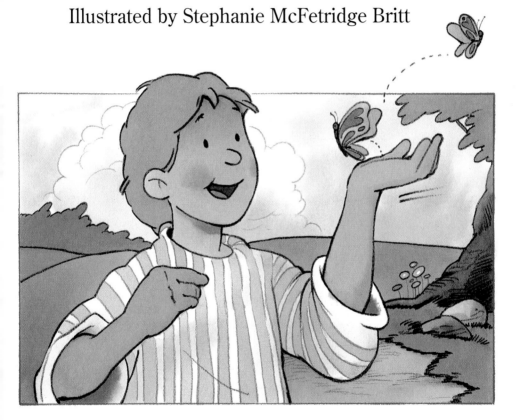

RAINBOW
STUDIES
INTERNATIONAL

Once there was a man
who had been blind
since he was born.
He had never seen anything
but darkness.

He loved the smell of warm *bread*,
but he did not know what bread looked like.

He could feel the silky fur of a *puppy*,
but he could not see a puppy.

He could hear the sweet song
of a *bird* outside his window,
but he had never seen a little bird.

Not even once.

One day, Jesus walked by.
He felt sorry for the blind man,
so He stopped to help.

Smoosh! The man felt cold, wet
mud on his eyes.
And then he heard the kindest voice
he had ever heard …
"Go to the pool and wash."

The man did not argue.
He just obeyed.

He went to the pool and washed his face.

Blink! Blink! Blink!
He opened his eyes wide.
He could see!

At last he could see blue *water*
and yellow and orange *fish*
and white *ducks* and red *flowers*

and green *frogs*
and purple *butterflies*
and anything else there was to see.

When the man came home seeing, his neighbors wanted to know how it happened.

The man told them that
Jesus had healed him.

But the people did not believe him.
They said terrible things about Jesus.

Then they sent the man away.

Jesus heard what the people
had said to the man.

So Jesus came to find him.

"Do you believe in
the Son of God?" Jesus asked.
The man wanted to know more.

"Tell me who He is so I can believe!"

"You are looking at Him," Jesus answered. And the man said, "Lord, I believe! I believe in You!"

"Listen," said the man to his neighbors,
"I have something to say.

Jesus, God's Son, healed me *twice* today!"

"My eyes were blind,
but now I *see*.

My heart was blind,
but now I *believe*."